BOSTON

A lone sculler on the Charles River.

BOSTON

HARRIS & ISOGAI

KODANSHA INTERNATIONAL LTD.
TOKYO, NEW YORK & SAN FRANCISCO

Distributors:
UNITED STATES: *Harper & Row, Publishers, Inc., 10 East 53rd Street, New York, New York 10022.* SOUTH AMERICA: *Harper & Row, International Department.* CANADA: *Fitzhenry & Whiteside Limited, 150 Lesmill Road, Don Mills, Ontario.* MEXICO AND CENTRAL AMERICA: *HARLA S.A. de C.V., Apartado 30–546, Mexico 4, D. F.* BRITISH COMMONWEALTH *(excluding Canada and the Far East): TABS, 7 Maiden Lane, London WC2.* EUROPE: *Boxerbooks Inc., Limmatstrasse 111, 8031 Zurich.* AUSTRALIA AND NEW ZEALAND: *Book Wise (Australia) Pty. Ltd., 104–8 Sussex Street, Sydney.* THAILAND: *Central Department Store Ltd., 306 Silom Road, Bangkok.* HONG KONG AND SINGAPORE: *Books for Asia Ltd., 30 Tat Chee Avenue, Kowloon; 65 Crescent Road, Singapore 15.* THE FAR EAST: *Japan Publications Trading Company, P.O. Box 5030, Tokyo International, Tokyo.*

Published by Kodansha International Ltd., 2-12-21 Otowa, Bunkyo-ku, Tokyo 112 and Kodansha International/USA, Ltd., 10 East 53rd Street, New York, New York 10022 and 44 Montgomery Street, San Francisco, California 94104. Copyright 1975 by Kodansha International Ltd. All rights reserved. Printed in Japan.

LCC 74-29567
ISBN 0-87011-244-9
JBC 0326-784780-2361

First edition, 1975

CONTENTS

"It still remains one of the few cities in America with an individuality and flavor entirely its own. It has never forgotten its past in terms of its present and to anyone who has lived in it long enough to know its ways, Boston is still, from a prejudiced viewpoint, one of the most satisfactory cities anywhere, and one of the most beguilingly beautiful."

John P. Marquand
Holiday, Nov. 1953

KALEIDOSCOPE

BOSTON, ON THE EAST COAST of the United States, is a city of seagulls on harbor wharves and pigeons fluttering from old, respected buildings. An intelligent place with a concentration of colleges and universities unparalleled in the country. A city of firsts—the first public school in America, first free public library, first public park, first subway. Once a very Protestant city with English family names, now largely a Catholic city with Irish and Italian names. Basically a genteel city, but occasionally a tough place with racial prejudice, snobbery, and violence.

A city with gentle summer ocean breezes and wild winter blizzards, frozen rivers, ice-covered sidewalks, piles of dirty snow—a seaport city with unexcelled seafood restaurants. It seems young in the green summer, older and tireder in the long New England winter.

To a visitor from Stockholm or even nearby Montreal, it may appear grimy; not so much a beautiful city as a city of beautiful parts. Its low skyline is broken by only a few medium-sized skyscrapers. A historic place where one *feels* the past, perhaps not as heavily as in Prague, but more than in Tokyo. Visitors are always finding bits and pieces of other cities here—London, San Francisco, Dublin, Paris. Its wide, park-lined Commonwealth Avenue could be the Champs-Elysées. Some of the South Boston bars could pass for Irish pubs. In other times, it was called "the Athens of America." Today, it is a city with a conscience. Unlike unzoned Texan cities which sprawl upon the plain and appear to have been built more with money than spirit, compact Boston possesses a self-assured balance between the old and the new. No American city except Philadelphia has so many historical buildings still standing, and its winding streets, which may once have been cowpaths, make it the easiest city in the country to get lost in.

Boston is not a booster's city where bigger and newer is automatically better. It is a big city with some small-town virtues, and the Chamber of Commerce knows its proper place. It is one of seven American cities still operating sensible trolley cars just as many European cities do. And its old burial grounds hold the remains of early colonists from England who moved into Boston over three hundred years ago. Boston, the home of several American Presidents.

It has been said that "a city does not merely consist of a lot of houses and buildings of different sizes, timber, and concrete, asphalt and green spots here and there. A city is a setting that human life there has created for itself—reflecting the temperament and mood of the inhabitants." And so Boston is a sensible place, a humane city on a human scale, a place of continuity which never forgets its past, above all a *livable* city (Mayor Kevin White's favorite adjective for Boston) with both faded elegance and garish modern.

Martin Luther King and Malcolm X both lived and studied here, and years after their deaths, Boston became the first major city in the north to be charged by the Federal Government (1971) with maintaining segregated schools. Boston, called the "Cradle of Liberty" and the home of abolitionism, is today a city with some racial prejudice. Cynics say it has less prejudice than before because most of the white Yankee self-proclaimed elite which once held Catholics and blacks in virtual subjection have fled the city for verdant suburbs, letting inner city residents fight it out among themselves. With almost three million people in the metropolitan area, Boston has the largest *percentage* of suburb-to-city commuters of any major American city.

Suburban Boston was my birthplace and boyhood home. Today, I live two hundred miles to the west, but still near enough for me to listen in to Boston radio stations and pick up newsstand copies of the *Boston Globe*.

Right away the reader will realize that I may not be able to write disinterestedly about Boston. Even if I were to pretend neutrality, some of my bias might show through and destroy the pose. Better for me to admit partiality and hope you can appreciate my enthusiasm. All the same I will try to be fair and see the city's faults as well as its virtues.

I have already used a word that best describes Boston—a *livable* city. The central city is so contained that a resident of Beacon Hill, an area near the state capitol, can easily walk in ten minutes to any of the following places: the theater district, with pre-Broadway plays; the Charles River Basin with sailing on the wide lagoon at the foot of Beacon Hill; the financial district; so-called Chinatown, with some fine restaurants; and the harbor which shaped Boston's early growth. Cities, as Boston writer Ian Menzies recently pointed out, have characteristics and personalities which make them as individual as people. Some depress us; others stimulate us. When a city reflects a harmonious blend of culture, history, and personal grace, then it sits comfortably with its peers—among them San Francisco, Florence, Copenhagen, London.

I feel that San Francisco and Boston, at opposite ends of the United States and each on a different ocean, are perhaps America's most interesting cities. Neither is so obsessed with progress that the past is disregarded. Both are self-aware and concerned: Bostonians are beginning to worry about the growing dimensions of their skyline at the very time San Franciscans are troubled about the "Manhattanization" of their skyline. Perhaps San Francisco, with its topless waitresses, all-nude dancers, and milder weather, has a freer spirit than sometimes constrained Boston, deeply rooted in a Puritanical past. But young, nomadic Americans are discovering Boston now, moving there in U-Haul trucks from all parts of the country and reshaping the city, altering its once stuffy image. It is fast becoming America's most youthful city. When I was a young student myself reading Thoreau, Emerson, and Holmes at college, I thought of Boston as a matronly, proper city, the staid Queen City of America's northeast. But now when I walk its vibrant streets surrounded by so many young people, I know Boston has the same youthful vigor as Munich.

While Boston may resemble other cities, in essence it is unique. Its climate alone would set it apart. Wintry storms which last for days and have the city digging out from several feet of snow immediately set it apart from London, Paris, or San Francisco. Its location on the east coast and its history give it a special place among American cities, for it was Boston which so sharply opposed British rule and was the cutting edge in the American Revolution when the colonies broke off from England and established their independent nation some two hundred years ago —in 1776.

It is the pace of the city that is so pleasant. By contrast, New York City, less than an hour away on one of the most heavily traveled air routes in the country, has a more hurried tempo: taxis seem to honk more and lurch through the streets faster. In the air of Manhattan one often feels tension, perhaps even stress— a vibrancy that for some is the tonic of New York.

Leave New York, take an air-shuttle flight to Boston, and note the difference right away, for Boston is a city of civility. Not that *all* Boston taxi drivers lining up for passengers at Logan International Airport are polite, but most of them have time for a brief "hello" before conversation gets around to destination. Perhaps I am obsessed with greetings, but I like to greet a taxi driver, a waiter, a hotel receptionist before getting down to business. In a New York taxi, I get a quick, "Where to?" or simply a jerk of the head indicating the same message without the effort of words. In Boston I always get a greeting. When I travel from one city to the other, I feel I'm bouncing between *yang* and *ying*, the frantic city and the gentle one.

The city is perhaps less gentle in winter, which always seems the longest of the four seasons. Like Montreal, which gets even more snow, Boston prepares for the fury of winter: storm doors are put up; hemp mats go down in store and office entrances to take the winter's snow and slush, the scraping of rubbers, over-shoes, or cleated boots. At Logan International Airport, giant plows are readied to keep the runways clear, for nobody knows when the first snows will come. And in the streets, Boston waits with smaller plows, road sanders and salters—never caught off guard, like Baltimore, where a few inches of snow at peak traffic time can all but paralyze the city.

In late fall, Boston weather forecasts are filled with references to sharp offshore winds and below-freezing temperatures; soon the word *snow* begins to sneak into these forecasts, first as "possible snow at higher elevations in the Berkshires," and then, as December settles in more firmly, as a more certain ingredient:

"Snow starting about midnight and continuing into mid-morning with expected accumulations of five to eight inches, possibly more in the suburbs and outlying areas." And the predicted snow comes, sifting down from the night sky, settling on the Public Garden, the wharves jutting into the quiet, gray harbor, the residential streets of Beacon Hill, the railyards, the pedestrian paths along the Charles River. It's a great time to walk around Boston in the soft, slanting snow of early December, knowing that it is a gentle storm compared with blizzards to come, knowing also that you are, after all those summer days of sun and autumn days of mild midday warmth, in one of America's northern most big cities and certain to experience cold.

The cruelest months are generally January and February when true winter blizzards are possible. Temperatures can hover for days around zero Fahrenheit and colder in the suburbs. The average winter snowfall is forty-two inches, but a few years ago 26.3 inches of snow fell on the city in five days. In the middle of winter, sidewalks may be glazed with ice; wind picks up speed over the harbor and bursts into the streets of the city, adding what meteorologists call "the wind chill factor" to the already low temperatures and numbing cold. Yet many a scarfed and gloved Bostonian has pride in coping unflappably with weather which would upset a Washingtonian.

Few Bostonians hibernate during the winter. Hardy music lovers can be seen in the severest winter storms making their way into Symphony Hall to hear the renowned Boston Symphony Orchestra, consistently one of the top symphonic orchestras in America. Members of the L Street Brownies, a South Boston "Polar Bear" club, are regularly photographed swimming among ice floes in the harbor. Joggers still jog along the banks of the Charles River, towels wrapped around necks. And workers in Boston offices can enjoy night skiing only a few miles south of the city in the Blue Hills. The big exodus, however, is on weekends when skiers head for the ski slopes of New Hampshire and Vermont, a few hours away. Until the energy squeeze hit the United States in 1974, most of these weekend ski trips were by car; gradually some buses, once discouraged at posh ski areas, are coming into use.

In theory, the severe winter *should* give way to a joyous spring when the city thaws out, renews itself among the budding flowers of the Public Garden and soft winds from off the Charles River, full of dinghys tacking in the gentle spring breeze. But, in fact, spring is sometimes a fleeting season in Boston. Chill winds may occasionally last until mid-April, when early baseball games have been canceled because of cold and rainy weather. Some years, spring seems to last only a few weeks, a brief transition between seasons. Two hundred miles to the south, New Yorkers may be strolling around Manhattan at noon enjoying the spring warmth while Bostonians are still wearing overcoats.

When the back of winter is finally broken, the city takes up its hemp doormats, sweeps sand and salt from its streets, and relaxes. Harvard and Radcliffe students lie on the banks of the Charles drinking wine, studying Chaucer, loving. Baseball fans, seated without shirts in the sunny bleachers of Fenway Park, root for their native Boston Red Sox baseball team, cheering for Boston most lustily when the New York Yankees are in town. No other team from any other major league city can attract the fans quite as much as the New York team, for a long-standing rivalry exists between the two cities. Nothing pleases a Bostonian more than to have the Red Sox defeat the New York Yankees. Boston is a great sports town with major league baseball, hockey, basketball, and football teams. As I write this, the Boston Celtics have just won the national basketball championship and the Bruins are competing in the playoff for the ice hockey championship. Bostonians are rightly proud of their professional teams and support them fully.

In the summer, the pace of Boston slows, especially on blistering days when the temperature is in the 90°'s; but there is escape from the heat, for Boston has a number of beaches within the city limits. While the water is generally safe, there are times when harbor pollution is high enough to discourage swimming at city beaches. Fortunately, the city is close to outlying beaches half an hour's travel away. Here, within view of the Boston skyline, one can sunbathe with surf rolling in from the open Atlantic.

It is in the summer, too, that Bostonians rediscover their harbor. A number of cruise boats, out of winter storage, ply the harbor on one-hour, three-hour, or half-day cruises. In fair weather, the one-hour harbor cruises are especially popular with office workers, who take a bag lunch and eat it in the harbor sunshine on a noontime cruise.

1–3. Boston is a city of the sea. *Opposite*, a dock worker spends lunch hour fishing; *below*, harbor shipping seen from Anthony's Pier 4 seaside restaurant. 4–5. Logan International Airport, the world's eighth busiest. Few major airports are as close to the center of the city.

6–7. Sailing is a year-round sport on the Charles River. *Opposite*, seen from the top of the Prudential Center, the river separates Boston from Cambridge and then winds its way inland.

8. Boston has the oldest subway system in the United States.

9. The city features many bookstores, for both new and used books, such as this one in the Old South Meeting House.

10. *Overleaf*, Commonwealth Avenue in the Back Bay section is a wide, parklike boulevard. The area was once a swamp but was filled in when nearby hills were lowered and now contains fine residences.

GOODSPEED'S BOOK SHOP, INC.
Old South Branch

GOODSPEED'S BOOK SHOP

GOODSPEED'S BOOK SHOP

11–14. Street scenes: *opposite above*, downtown School Street; *others*, Newbury Street with elegant shops and outdoor restaurant terraces.

15. *Overleaf*, Boston has many antique shops. This one is on "The Freedom Trail," a walkable few blocks of historical interest.

16. *Opposite*, Old South Meeting House, built in 1729.

17–19. Illustrations from the Tea Party Museum recall the early great shipping days of Boston.

20. The State House: Boston is the largest state capital city in all fifty states.

21. *Overleaf*, Beacon Hill, an area of fashionable residences and town houses, has retained most of its historic charm.

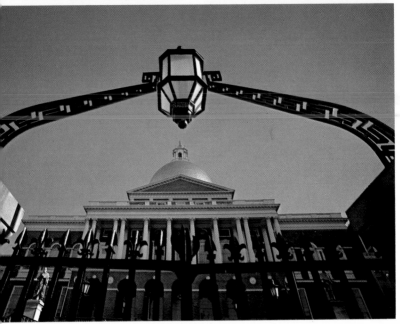

PURITANS AND SUCCESSORS

It is, perhaps, unjust to say that the first settlement of Boston occurred in 1630. The idea that the history of Boston can only be dated from the arrival of expatriates determined to find freedom away from England is a narrow one, for the original settlers were North American Indians. Eventually they were uprooted and displaced by white settlers. Today, about all that remains of the Indian civilization are place names around Boston—Neponset, Swampscott, Mattapan, Shawmut. Shawmut was the original Indian name for pre-colonial Boston, a word kept alive today by one of Boston's largest banks.

It was the Indians who taught the early arrivals from England how to survive in cold Plymouth, just south of Boston where the first English lived. They came on the *Mayflower* from Plymouth, England, and in their wooden-frame, thatched, pitched-roof houses they were the first permanent settlers from across the Atlantic.

A decade later, in 1630, John Winthrop and Richard Saltonstall landed north of Boston in Salem, then moved to a small peninsula in Boston harbor between the Mystic and the Charles rivers in an area now known as the Charlestown section of Boston.

The early settlers encamped on a hilly peninsula surrounded by water where several rivers emptied into the Atlantic. They were not really maritime folk; most of them had had enough of the sea on long crossings of the Atlantic from Britain. They had come to this place to *escape*, to get away from their own country for a variety of reasons, including a desire for religious freedom. Puritanical, mostly Congregational, these first colonists were prepared to cope with a new land, harsher winters than even Scotland experienced, and whatever came along.

Nevertheless, Boston developed as a maritime city with wharves and shipyards. Inhabited by so many natives of London, the city developed into a microcosm of the European capital. An early historian remarked that conversation was as polite as in the towns and cities of England "so that a Gentleman from London would almost think of himself at home in Boston."

By the end of the seventeenth century, Boston had truly become a major seaport. Its vessels ranked third in the English-speaking world and it embarked on trade which soon became worldwide. Yet Boston was a maze of narrow, crooked streets and little byways which connected shops and taverns. The city's name was English, too, taken from Boston or St. Botolph's Town in Lincolnshire. Scores of town and city names around Boston are borrowed from English towns. In this age of jet travel, occasional residents of, say, Winchester, will include England's Winchester in their European tour, not simply to see the cathedral, but to revel in the ancient English town which gave their suburb its name.

Early Boston was quite hilly—almost as hilly as San Francisco is today. Some of these hills remain today—Beacon Hill, Copp's Hill, Fort Hill—but they have been considerably scaled down, for the tops were leveled off to fill in coves and nearby marshy land. In fact, the flat, largely residential area of Boston called Back Bay was an early landfill project created from nearby hills!

Unfortunately, few of the early buildings of Boston remain

today. The only seventeenth-century building that has survived is the Paul Revere House, so called because silversmith and midnight rider Paul Revere lived there for a while. Like most of Boston's *really* old buildings, this house is to be found in the North End section near the harbor. In 1676 a wide-ranging fire swept through this area and the present Paul Revere House was rebuilt after the fire. Nearby is The Old South Meeting House (1729), another remnant of this early settlement.

As everyone knows, tension between the colony and England grew. The colonists, accustomed to their new liberty, objected to higher taxes on imported items, especially a tax on tea. A shipment of tea was dumped into Boston harbor and gave rise to the world's best-known party—the Boston Tea Party. Later, when English troops were sent "to cow the rebellious subjects," a brief but famous war ensued—the American Revolution. When a Declaration of Independence was enacted in 1776, an independent nation had been established. Thus, the year 1976 is an important date in Boston and America—the 200th anniversary of the nation's birth, a time when Americans will be reminded that their nation was born in protest and revolution. Boston will have no great bicentennial plans except to offer the city itself as an architectural and historic exhibit.

Until the middle of the nineteenth century, Boston was largely a Protestant and English city. With its writers, literary magazines, and effete manners, it was the cultural center of the United States. But in a rough new country, Boston's dignified posture seemed pompous, and when the Irish potato famine caused rural Irish farmers to set sail for Boston in large numbers, stiff-backed Bostonians and Irish immigrants formed an uneasy duality. Who were these Irish farmers settling into the North End, opening their own schools, saloons, coal yards—and even running for political office? The unyielding prejudice which greeted these

Irish-Catholic immigrants is not a pleasant chapter in Boston's history. Later prejudice against Italian immigrants and also French Canadians who crossed the border from Quebec was even worse, since neither group spoke English.

Protestant intolerance became outspoken, for all these immigrants were Catholics who soon established churches, parish schools, and convents against every sort of local obstacle—curious, since the original English settlers came largely for their own religious freedom. One would have thought they could tolerate someone else's religion.

By the time of America's civil war, the city had its first Catholic college—Boston College—and not many years later its first Irish mayor, Hugh O'Brien. The city's police department soon became largely Irish and Italian, and today (with many a "proper Bostonian" having moved to suburban Wayland or Dedham) Boston is considered an Irish-Italian city, despite the obvious fact that its citizens are, above all, Americans. Yet pockets of Protestant prejudice still exist, even though Boston gave America its first Irish-Catholic President, John F. Kennedy, who once campaigned for political office in the wards of Boston.

Boston grew as a shipping center primarily because of its protected, island-ringed harbor. Shipbuilding was a major industry. Vigorous trade was carried on with the West Indies, with the Canary Islands, Mediterranean ports and eventually with China. Boston imported sugar, cotton, oil, molasses, wines, and exported dried fish, lumber, rum and flour. Eventually, the port fell behind Philadelphia and New York as far as major shipping went, but it remained the main fishing port on the east coast with tons of fresh fish brought in daily from Atlantic waters.

Increasingly, Boston turned to textiles. Huge textile plants were built along New England rivers. Importing cotton and wool, these mills turned out much of America's finished cloth.

In fact, until fairly recently Boston was known as the wool capital of the world. But as southern states grew and offered cheaper labor and a milder climate, much of the textile business moved south, especially to the Carolinas nearer the source of cotton. Today Greater Boston is filled with huge old brick buildings which were once textile mills. Some have become bottling plants, warehouses, factory outlet stores. Others sit at river's edge, broken-windowed and abandoned, reminders of a textile industry that decamped and moved to warmer climes.

No history of Boston during this period, however brief, could ignore the city's widespread fame as a literary center. Longfellow, Lowell, Whittier, Emerson, Thoreau, Holmes, Parkman, Alcott, Hawthorne—the list of Boston writers is formidable and plenty of publishers existed also, as well as literary magazines such as *The Atlantic Monthly* and the *North American Review*. Certain cities at certain times in their history have a radiating influence on civilization, and this is true of Boston's literary effect on America during the nineteenth century. Unfortunately, Boston took all this too seriously, fawning on its writers. In truth, Henry Wadsworth Longfellow was not much of a poet, but what a figure he cut when he dined at the Parker House, esteemed there as a poet, linguist, professor! Other cities might have lavished praise on bridge builders or army generals, but Boston exalted the writers in its midst.

Respecting writers rather than warriors would ordinarily be harmless enough, but in Boston the genteel tradition was so prized that too many Boston writers excluded from their work feelings of deeply personal truths; an obsession with manners interfered with their art. As visiting British professor Martin Green observed in *The Problem of Boston*: "The New England feeling prevented literary people from thinking about or writing about the feelings that mattered most to them and their audience.

So they wrote about things that did not matter too much." Thus, Oliver Wendell Holmes was bringing out *The Professor at the Breakfast Table* and *Over the Teacups* at a time when Walt Whitman, two hundred miles south in New York, was coming to terms with his sensuality in *Leaves of Grass*, a book soon banned in Boston. Ultimately many Boston book publishers moved to New York, which quickly became the publishing capital of the country. Boston's writers were soon eclipsed by non-New England writers like Willa Cather or Theodore Dreiser.

Fortunately, Boston's literary history does not end on this note, for with writers such as John P. Marquand (*The Late George Apley*) and Gerald Warner Brace (*The Garretson Chronicle*) the transition from suffocating reverence to modern realism was accomplished. For anyone interested in contemporary Boston, I would recommend two novelists: Edwin O'Connor and George V. Higgins. O'Connor in two superb novels, *The Last Hurrah* and *The Edge of Sadness* (which won the Pulitzer Prize in 1962), came to terms with Irish-American politics and life in Boston; he examined the inward-looking, almost claustrophobic preoccupations of Catholicism in this very Catholic city. George V. Higgins has chronicled Boston's underworld of petty criminals in *The Friends of Eddie Coyle, The Digger's Game*, and *Cogan's Trade*.

Boston's publishing output today is indeed small compared with New York, but the quality is high. Two prestigious firms, Little Brown and Houghton Mifflin (which once published Longfellow, Whittier, and Hawthorne), produce strong lists, along with Beacon Press and a number of university presses, such as Harvard and Massachusetts Institute of Technology (better known as M.I.T.). *The Atlantic Monthly*, founded over a century ago, is still published in Boston.

In recent years Boston has been considered more as an electronics center than a literary place. Massachusetts Institute of Technology has led the way in the city's emergence as a modern center of science and electronics. A circular highway around Boston, Route 128, is today filled with electronic research and manufacturing firms; no longer are textiles, leather tanning, and shoemaking the focus of Boston industry.

LANDMARKS

If you were to visit Boston, the chances are you would not arrive by train or ship. That's still possible, unless yet another railroad station is torn down before this book is in print, but most visitors arrive by air, landing at Logan International Airport, the eighth-busiest airport in the world. Ten trans-Atlantic airlines fly nonstop from such European cities as London, Rome, Zürich, Frankfurt, and Paris to Boston's airport, which is several hundred miles nearer European cities than New York. Airport officials from Boston, in fact, make annual trans-Atlantic pilgrimages to induce European travel agents to book European visitors to America through Boston as a gateway city, and their efforts are paying off. Increasingly, European tourists are using Boston as their first American port of call.

Flying in from Europe, your aircraft will skim over Labrador and Newfoundland at its assigned altitude, but over the state of Maine, the most northeastern state, the plane will shift to progressively lower altitudes. Soon you will see the New England coastline, rocky at first, then with occasional sandy beaches as Maine gives way to New Hampshire and Massachusetts. On a clear day, fishing vessels will be visible off the coast. If you are low enough to see markings, you may notice that many of these ships are Russian, for the modern state-supported Russian fleets have been taking huge catches from New England waters in recent years—to the dismay of Massachusetts fishing ports such as Boston, Gloucester, and New Bedford.

Then, at an elevation of about five thousand feet, you will fly over two historic sea towns north of Boston, Salem and Marblehead. By the time you sweep over the beaches and lobster boats of Swampscott, my home town, flight attendants will be seated and seat-belts fastened for the landing approach.

As your jet drifts in a wide arc over Boston harbor to line up with a long runway, you will notice the many harbor islands below. For too many years, these splendid islands have been neglected. Some have been abandoned with only the remnants of a military fort left, others put to work as sewage plant, prison, hospital. With rats on some islands and polluted waters washing up debris, the islands look more attractive from the air than close up. Fortunately, a group of concerned Bostonians has realized that these harbor islands, so close to Boston and yet so remote, are a valuable asset, and plans are underway to clean them up and develop a master plan for their intelligent use—for recreation, for harbor living, as well as for historic preservation. No one can predict the exact future for Georges, Calf, or Gallops Islands, to name three of the twenty-eight harbor islands now remaining, but it is certain they face a promising future.

You may be surprised when you step outside the air terminal to see the skyline of Boston so close, just a mile or two distant across harbor water. In fact, the length of the longest runway is more than the distance from the terminal area to Boston's City Hall! Few major world airports are as close to the central city as this one, an eight- to twelve-minute taxi ride to the center of the city. Shuttle buses also connect up with the airport's subway stop (appropriately named *Airport*) in the oldest subway system in the United States.

Logan International Airport is in a part of the city called East Boston. If I were to meet you and drive you into the center of the city, we'd probably take a tunnel under the river, for downtown Boston, jutting out like a peninsula, is surrounded by water on three sides and is approachable mainly via bridges or tunnels. Commuters from the suburbs jam these approaches morning and evening. In the summer of 1973 a single truck accident during heavy morning traffic on the huge two-level Mystic River Bridge resulted in a massive traffic jam that lasted for four and a half hours.

Emerging from Sumner tunnel, we would find ourselves in the midst of the city and not far from good hotels. Not too many years ago you might have stayed reasonably in one of Boston's venerable hotels, perhaps the Hotel Vendome in the Back Bay section which was largely residential, wealthy, and, unlike most of Boston, arranged in a rectangular network of streets. The Vendome, with its richly paneled public rooms and bright Oriental rugs on gleaming floors, would have been a very "proper" address—in a city that has at times been obsessed with propriety.

But now the beautiful old hotel, with a modern addition which blends in as well as possible, is a residential hotel and apartment complex. In preserving its architectural past, Boston has simply recycled its older buildings, so that a onetime firehouse becomes a townhouse, a warehouse becomes an apartment building, a church turns into a theater, and a newspaper building where once the presses rolled is converted into an office building much in demand by business people who *prefer* the old to the new, whose spirits are actually *lifted* by working in an old building where electricity was installed years *after* construction and where the windows actually open.

Not all Boston's landmarks are old, however; the city contains an interesting amalgam of architectural moods. Among the places I would recommend visiting are the following:

The Prudential Center

For many years the best view of Boston was from the tower of the city's twenty-five-story Custom House near the harbor. But new construction techniques have made it possible (although very expensive) to anchor tall buildings in the soft soil of Boston and so the Prudential Insurance Company of America erected a fifty-two-story building in the midst of a complex of offices, restaurants, and stores in Boston's Back Bay on land reclaimed from a swamp. Today the Skywalk on the fiftieth floor of this building offers an unparalleled view of Boston and surrounding areas. On a clear day you can see the outline of New Hampshire mountains, some eighty miles away.

Naturally these mountains, or even nearby suburbs, are not visible on days when industrial haze hangs over the city, although Boston's sea breezes help to lessen its air pollution problem. On such a day the view may be limited to the roofs of Back Bay homes and offices, or to what lies just beyond—the Charles River Basin and America's prestigious technical university, Massachusetts Institute of Technology in Cambridge. A six-lane highway can be seen running parallel to the river; this was constructed despite impassioned objections, but strips of land next to the water were left for walking, jogging, and bicycling, with pedestrian bridges over the Storrow Drive and its heavy traffic flow.

The John Hancock Building

The view east of the harbor and Logan International Airport is dominated by an even taller building, the John Hancock Insurance Building, probably the most controversial building ever constructed in Boston. At sixty-two stories it is the tallest in

Boston and has been plagued by an incredible number of problems. As I write, it is still unoccupied—long after the date for its scheduled completion—and many an architect's lip has curled in reference to this beleaguered building, designed by I. M. Pei and partners. The chief executive of the insurance company which built the structure had to explain to stockholders in January, 1974, that all the windows in the building, many of which had been broken, cracked, or sucked out by wind and had been temporarily replaced with plywood, would have to be replaced at a cost of five or six million dollars. For some reason, the $750 Thermoplane windows of insulating glass originally installed could not stand up to the pressure of air currents and mysteriously popped, sending showers of glass down below. The new windows will be of reflective but not insulating glass, making the building, already anathema to ecologists, more wasteful in terms of heating fuel.

The problems this building endured may have been beneficial in the long run, for they have focused the attention of Bostonians on the inappropriateness of tall buildings in the low profile of the city. As I said earlier, Bostonians, like citizens of San Francisco, are reevaluating the concept of tall buildings which block views, create long shadows, change even street-level wind currents, and burn up enormous amounts of energy. Quite possibly these two rival insurance buildings may be the highest structures on Boston's skyline for some years to come.

Beacon Hill

Some cities are monotonously flat, but not Boston. Best known of its many hills is Beacon Hill in downtown Boston. It has lost little of its charm through the years, although its north-slope houses have been chopped up into rental apartments for X-ray technicians, nurses, and doctors who appreciate its closeness to

Massachusetts General Hospital. The hill's sunny side facing Boston Common is still elegant. Here on Beacon, Acorn, Walnut, Cedar, and Chestnut Streets are fine old houses in the architectural style of the Georgian Federalist period. Perhaps the purple glass has changed color through the years, an airconditioner may protrude from an upper-floor bedroom, or an iron mud-scraper on an outside step may have disappeared, but the area has not deteriorated as many neighborhoods have. Through the determined efforts of many a Beacon Hill matron who staged rocking chair sit-ins on its brick streets and sidewalks, concrete paving has not replaced car-jarring brick on much of the Hill.

Many travelers have noted how cobblestoned Louisburg Square resembles parts of South Kensington in London. In fact, two American movies supposedly with a London locale were actually filmed around Beacon Hill. Here and there among the townhouses are a few restaurants or small offices. The western edge of Beacon Hill bordering on Charles Street is filled with antique shops.

On top of Beacon Hill is the state capitol building. Few American states have their capitals located in their largest city, but Boston is an exception. In fact, it is the largest capital city of all fifty states. The gold-leafed State House dominates the view for miles around, especially for boaters on the Charles River. Hanging in the State House is the sacred codfish, suspended as "a reminder of the importance of Cod Fishing for the welfare of the Commonwealth." The building was designed by Charles Bulfinch, a Boston-born architect who saw his work completed in 1795 when he was just thirty-two and who is responsible for many buildings around Boston.

Government Center
In the midst of downtown Boston, this complex of buildings and

plazas is impossible to miss. It would be an oversimplification to say that the sixty-one-acre center is a result of urban renewal, for that term implies a vast tearing-down of old buildings in order to erect something new. True, the present site of Government Center was once Scollay Square, a disaster area of cheap bars, tatoo parlors, souvenir shops. It even housed a burlesque theater, The Old Howard Athenaeum where some of us as Harvard undergraduates would go on a Saturday night to see the newest tassle-queen, the "direct from the Folies Bergère" stripper, or those baggy-pants vaudeville stars who made so many local jokes.

A mixture of the past and the present is what makes Government Center so attractive. The Boston Redevelopment Authority determined from the beginning that historic old buildings had to be incorporated in the master plan. So old buildings like Faneuil Hall, Sears Crescent, and the Old State House coexist with new structures, including a stunning new City Hall with a nine-acre plaza, and a Federal building named after President Kennedy, all designed around a huge, open, warm brick plaza with plenty of room to stroll, sun, or have a picnic lunch. There are stairways and fountains and benches. So much of the old has remained mixed in and surrounding the new that one is caught between centuries. A friend and I were seated last spring at an outdoor restaurant in front of the nineteenth-century Sears Crescent, looking alternately at the twentieth-century buildings near us and the eighteenth-century Faneuil Hall nearby. We couldn't help but remark on how the centuries blended into one another in this part of Boston.

What ultimately distinguishes Government Center is that it was designed for the pedestrian. For once cars seem to rate lower on the scale. John Fischer, an editor of *Harper's* magazine published in New York City, was so impressed by the area that he wrote, "Boston has now become, in fact, one of the few American cities where a stroll through the downtown business district is a pleasure rather than an ordeal."

Boston Common and Public Garden

Most American cities have public parks in their midst, but Boston has the distinction of having the oldest. Early English residents purchased in 1634 (for a mere thirty pounds) some forty-five acres from a hermit and established the public land for grazing.

Today the Common is used for strolling, dog walking, bag lunches, baseball, ice skating, sun bathing, and massive political demonstrations. Beneath it is a huge underground garage. Additional acreage reclaimed from swampy land became the Public Garden, separated from the Common by Charles Street. Here, too, are paths for walking, trees for shade or nature study (most trees are identified by explanatory signs), an artificial lake with pedal boats called Swan Boats.

To be honest, both the Common and the Public Garden have seen better days. A *Boston Globe* writer recently lamented the present state of these two adjacent pieces of land in an article entitled, "The Decline and Probable Fall of Boston Common and the Public Garden." The journalist noted that the Common's Frog Pond hadn't seen a frog in many a year. The pond, drained most of the time, has accumulated bottles, beer cans, and wind-blown newspapers. Graffiti mar statues, fences have been vandalized. Gone is the deer park, a greenhouse, and a small aquarium. The Garden, too, has suffered: plants have been ripped up, railings damaged by cars, and an expanding dog population leaves remains everywhere in the Garden and spoils the grass.

A few years ago a Boston official returned from a European visit impressed with how European urban specialists have found aesthetically pleasing solutions to practical problems. Determined to meet the Common's graffiti problem, he had an official

"Graffiti Board" put up in the park. At first it was filled with obscenities. Painted over, religion and poetry then appeared. Finally it was the philosopher's turn: "Apathy is the greatest problem in America; but who cares?"

Boston Public Library

To some, the finest building in all Boston is the Public Library which faces Copley Square. Simple in its horizontal line, classical in style, light in color (though darkened by time), this magnificent Italian Renaissance building designed by Charles McKim faces east. Inside is not only oak paneling, but an arcaded courtyard. Because of its proximity to a number of colleges, notably Northeastern and Boston Universities, it is patronized by large numbers of students. In cold months, some of Boston's homeless men in shabby overcoats linger over newspapers in its heated reading room.

Long overcrowded with books and students, the library recently expanded into a new wing, a $24,000,000 ten-story structure which abuts the original building. Architectural magazines have hailed the functional new wing because it blends in so compatibly. There's a reason—granite for the addition came from the same Milford quarry which supplied the original 1895 building. The quarry had been abandoned, but it was reopened to serve this specific function.

The Christian Science Church Center

Boston is the world headquarters of Christian Science, and some twenty-five acres near the center of Boston have been devoted to a church-housing-publishing complex. Architect I. M. Pei has created a plaza with an enormous pool of water. Around this plaza is the church edifice itself and the printing plant which daily publishes the worldwide daily newspaper, *The Christian Science*

Monitor. Nearly all architectural magazines have extolled the virtues of this complex, pointing out the grandeur and sweep of the design, still well integrated into the city itself.

Despite its beauty, especially at night with lights reflecting in the pool, the complex has been criticized for the way tenants were moved out under urban renewal. Some feel the Center was erected as a secure enclave of wealth insulated from the deteriorating, visually distracting neighborhood surrounding the property. There are even some who say the project is barren, self-involved, perhaps even pompous, but each visitor must decide alone.

For years I've been advising people to visit the Center's Mapparium, and nobody has ever been disappointed. Essentially it is a huge walk-in globe, though its impact is hard to describe. As you walk inside, around you is the world in hundreds of brightly lit panels, and though as a child I spent hours in this Mapparium, it has remained a favorite haunt of mine.

The Museum of Science

Standing beside a lock where the murky Charles River empties into the inner harbor, this museum was designed to be, and surely is, *participatory*. Here one can see how things work—the body, radar, gravity. Exhibitions are arranged so that visitors can manipulate, touch, and turn. What's more, demonstrations are always being put on—of snakes, porcupines, beavers. And the museum's Hayden Planetarium is appropriate to a city which has had so many well-known astronomers.

The Gardner Museum

This is an off-beat museum with a novel history. An exceedingly colorful Bostonian, Isabella Stewart Gardner, had it built in her honor in what had been the Fenway swamps of Boston, now an attractive parklike area. The building, not especially distinguished on the outside, has a skylit courtyard with flowers from its own greenhouse. The museum houses the founder's personal collection. According to her will, no new acquisitions were to be brought in, no admission charge was ever to be made, and the director was to live in private quarters on the fourth floor. These conditions all prevail today just as they did when the museum was opened in 1902.

The Boston Museum of Fine Arts

A handsome collection of Impressionists, the leading Oriental collection in the country, and exhibitions of the highest quality make this museum a supremely worthwhile visit. As I write this, the Museum is having an exhibition of rare works from 2600 years of American art with rare Olmec ceramics and jades and ancient Aztec and Inca art; most of the exhibits came from private collections around Boston and New England.

Combat Zone

Once, sailors from ships that put in to the Boston Navy Yard headed immediately for Scollay Square and its bars, burlesque shows, and nightclubs. But owing to urban renewal, Scollay Square exists no more; even the subway station once called Scollay has been renamed Government Center. At night the area is quiet, for the action has shifted a few blocks away down on Washington Street near its intersection with Boylston Street, where pornographic bookstores, seamy bars, cafes with strippers, and "X"-rated movies are common enough. Prostitutes of both sexes, drug pushers, and occasional muggers are attracted here and operate in what is informally called Boston's "Combat Zone."

Hardly as famous as Hamburg's Reeperbahn with its government-sanctioned Palace of Love, the Combat Zone is an amazing place considering Boston's long history of civic prudery. Until only a few years ago, certain books and plays were regularly banned in the city "for their frankness." Boston seems to accept its Combat Zone in the belief that it is better to contain vice in one area than to cause it to spread by attempting to eliminate it altogether.

The North End

The North End is a densely populated area of the city near the harbor wharves and the confluence of the Charles and Mystic Rivers. In no other American city except Philadelphia are so many colonial sites still standing. Here, despite TV aerials, late-model cars, and airconditioners, one can feel the streets and byways of the early seaport. Even though a highway thrusts through the neighborhood, the North End has a cohesive community atmosphere, perhaps because after successive waves of immigrants, it has accepted its identity as an Italian-American section of Boston. Italian is widely spoken throughout the area, shops carry imported items from Italy, and the Feast of St. Anthony is annually celebrated with pageantry and good humor.

In too many American cities, public vegetable and fruit markets have disappeared, but not in Boston's North End where crates of produce are sold on several market days at the end of the week. In season, vegetables sold in Haymarket Square are truly "farm fresh," having been trucked in from farms thirty or forty miles away.

With its old streets and buildings, its ancient but neglected burial ground on Copp's Hill, its nautical flavor, and its fine but unassuming restaurants, the North End happens to be my favorite section of Boston.

Filene's Basement

Several years ago when city mayors (all men!) from all over the United States were meeting in Boston, their wives were getting acquainted with the city. Asked later what places they liked, they invariably named Filene's basement. It isn't historic, being simply the basement of a seventy-year-old department store on Washington Street, but its fame has spread. For here, if you're lucky, you might pick up an Yves St. Laurent silk blouse reduced from its original $90 selling price at I. Magnin to a basement price of $16.95.

Filene's basement is unique. Its thirty buyers often purchase huge stocks from stores going out of business, or else manufacturers' surplus or even "castoffs" from well-known American stores in other cities—Bonwit's, Saks Fifth Avenue, Neiman-Marcus, Bergdorf Goodman. Every article is tagged with a price, often a third of its original one, and the date it went on sale. After twelve sales days it is automatically reduced 25% in price. After six more days, there's another 25% reduction, and again another 25% after six more days. If the article hasn't sold in thirty days, it's shipped off to charity.

As you can imagine, some incredible bargains turn up in Filene's basement, a place patronized by a true cross section of society. Here college professors from Harvard finger the suit racks along with off-duty postal workers. Many a well-to-do Brookline resident has cheerfully admitted that an article of clothing with a label from the faraway Neiman-Marcus store in Texas was actually bought at Filene's basement. Fortunately, many Bostonians have the kind of security which allows them not only to save money this way but to boast about their good fortune.

Some male voyeurs claim the woman's clothing section of Filene's basement is the best peep show in town as women sometimes try on dresses or slips right in the crowded aisles. I don't know; I've been too busy shopping in the men's department, where, over the years, I've purchased suits, ties, shirts, and sports jackets with store labels from cities like Omaha that I've never even visited.

Harvard University

Again, it is hard for me to write disinterestedly about Harvard, for the University has been a family tradition for generations. I tried to break the pattern by applying for admission to Dartmouth, a woodsy outdoor college in New Hampshire. But Dartmouth rejected me and I ended up, after all, at my father's and grandfather's alma mater, the oldest college in the United States (founded in 1636) and the college which has graduated more American Presidents than any other—three in the twentieth century alone: both Roosevelts as well as John Fitzgerald Kennedy.

The Harvard campus, a few miles from downtown Boston, sprawls over acres in both Boston and Cambridge, on opposite sides of the Charles River. The undergraduate college is mostly in Cambridge, but several of the graduate schools and most outdoor athletic facilities are in Boston. The oldest buildings at Harvard, including Massachusetts Hall built in 1720, are on the campus called Harvard Yard, along with the largest university library in the United States, Widener Library, the second-largest library of any sort in the country.

A visitor to London has to go a good bit out of his way to reach either Oxford or Cambridge, but Harvard is ten minutes by subway from midtown Boston. Unlike the subway to the airport which tunnels under the harbor, the subway to Harvard emerges from underground before leaving Boston, crosses the Charles River, and returns underground for the end of the line. University buildings are less than fifty yards from the station.

On several acres of subway yards just beyond Harvard Square is the site of a proposed Memorial to the late President Kennedy. Just a few months before his death in Texas, President Kennedy personally chose a library site on the Boston side of the Charles River, but as plans for a useful, functional center developed, it became clear that a larger site was needed. As I write this, revised plans for the Kennedy Library have been submitted, but construction will not start until objections, especially from Cambridge residents who fear massive traffic snarls, have been overcome. Once the center is completed, hopefully for America's bicentennial in 1976, it is expected to be a far more utilitarian study and historical center than, for example, the library in Texas devoted to the presidential papers of Lyndon Johnson.

THE BATTLE OF LEXINGTON

22–26. Many cities might destroy an old city hall when a new one is built. But this Old City Hall (*preceding page*) was restored and converted into offices and a restaurant. Nearby, an immense plaza contains the new City Hall and a Federal Building named after John F. Kennedy, once a Boston Congressman. Government Center Plaza is ideal for noontime sunning.

27. *Overleaf*, the view from the Parker House Hotel shows new construction in the heart of downtown Boston.

28–32. While Boston has its share of gleaming new hotels, the venerable Parker House is still popular for lodging or morning coffee. Seafood is common in Boston restaurants such as the Union Oyster House, *below*, and Anthony's Pier 4, *overleaf*.

33. *Preceding page*, Boston Common, once a grazing ground for neighborhood cattle, has now become an open recreational area in the center of the city. Underneath is a huge parking garage.

34–35. Children love Franklin Park, a few miles from the commercial center of the city. It also contains a small zoo.

36. *Below*, kite sailing at a golf course near Franklin Park.

37–38. *Preceding and opposite pages*, the Public Garden, a pastoral setting in the midst of the city, is famed for its Swan Boats—foot-pedaled vessels which cruise a placid four-acre pond.

39–41. A recent addition to this maritime city is the New England Aquarium, with several tanks three stories high.

42. *Below*, splashers at the Frog Pond in Boston Common.

43–45. Boston's Museum of Science, in the Charles River Basin, is noted for its lively, participatory exhibits.
46. *Overleaf,* Boston Public Library, the oldest free library in the country and one of Boston's most magnificent buildings.

47. *Opposite*, the courtyard of the Isabella Stewart Gardner Museum reminds one of a Venetian *palazzo* of another century. Just off the courtyard are paintings by Whistler, Sargent and Matisse.

48–49. Boston is the headquarters of Christian Science. The Mother Church, offices and the publishing company which issues an international daily newspaper are located in a spectacular plaza designed by I. M. Pei.

50. The Museum of Fine Arts is known for its Oriental collection and Egyptian murals. American artists are also represented.

BOSTON'S PRIDE

Boston Brahmins

For most of its existence, Boston has been a class-conscious city with a stuffy upper class which felt superior not only to the rest of Boston, but to people elsewhere in America. Essentially of white Anglo-Saxon Protestant ancestry, "Proper Bostonian" WASPS have been obsessed with family lineage.

The provincialism of this fading Boston aristocracy has long been an object of humor. A Beacon Hill lady is supposed to have declined the idea of travel with the comment, "Why should I travel when I'm already there?" Perhaps too many Bostonians believed their city was the hub of the universe. As for the rest of America, well, it was simply a large blank area to the west in which Dayton, Kansas City, Toledo, Tulsa, Milwaukee and other such cities were located. Intolerant of newer and crasser cities, the "Proper Bostonian" felt uncomfortable even in New York. At the age of eighty, Boston businessman Charles Francis Adams always managed to return home on a milk train rather than stay overnight in New York.

These aristocratic WASP families were named Forbes, Adams, Lowell, Cabot, Winthrop, Appleton, Sears, Thayer, and Saltonstall. Although they lived well, often on Beacon Hill, they were characteristically unostentatious, believing in sensible clothing and distrusting whatever was suddenly new and "in." Cleveland Amory, who has chronicled Boston's aristocracy in *Proper Bostonians*, recounts that for the traditional Bostonian lady "the more chic and modern the store the more irritated it makes her." Likewise, it is said that Thomas Perkins, a Boston shipping merchant, had a leather thong attached to his gold watch. A Boston jeweler once made the mistake of suggesting that, considering Mr. Perkins' position, he might want a gold watch chain. Perkins replied that his position was such that he could perfectly well afford to wear a leather thong.

This self-possession is still shown by the families of well-entrenched Bostonians today. Sometimes outstripped financially by *nouveaux riches* contractors who drive only big new cars, secure Bostonians take an almost perverse pride in driving ordinary cars, wearing comfortable and occasionally frayed clothing, and resisting whatever may be temporarily in fashion, whether doubleknit suits or boots to replace perfectly good laced shoes. Many a Boston businessman today wears a winter topcoat with a Leopold Morse label, yet the store went out of business more than a dozen years ago!

Fortunately, Boston society, once so highly structured and obsessed with genealogical distinctions, is changing with the times. As recently as a decade ago, girls from prominent families made their formal debuts, flitted from one debutante party to another, married Harvard law school graduates and, after tours of Europe, settled down to being the wives of rising lawyers in Boston law firms. Now there are fewer debutantes, cotillions, teas—less desire to conform to family and social traditions. Today the daughter of a prominent white Anglo-Saxon Protestant Bostonian may well be an ardent, jeans-wearing feminist vociferously opposed to the old, crumbling aristocracy. As Alison Arnold observed recently, there is now a certain status in *not* having a debut. Perhaps the money saved could go for a really worthwhile project—a drug counseling program, a meditation center, or a food cooperative. Boston society is not dead; the *Social Register* still publishes its listings of properly acceptable people. But in a city with so many concerned activists, an elaborate social life today seems irrelevant, or worse.

Indeed, Boston is rapidly gaining a reputation as one of America's more liberal cities. Few cities in America turned out such huge crowds in opposition to the Viet Nam war as Boston, where gatherings of 100,000 protesters on Boston Common were not unusual. Boston also voted overwhelmingly against President Nixon in 1972, and Massachusetts had the distinction of being the only state to reject Nixon and vote for his Democratic opponent, Senator George McGovern. A year or two later when food prices soared, vast corruption in Washington was uncovered, gasoline was in short supply, and unemployment was growing along with dissatisfaction with Nixon, occasional Boston automobiles sported the bumper sticker: "Don't blame me, I'm from Massachusetts."

Despite its long-held image as a genteel city of learning and culture, Boston in truth has long been an activist center. Once the key city in America's opposition to English rule, then later a center of abolition, Boston has attracted a reputation as an anti-war city. Many Bostonians opposed the War of 1812 and the Mexican War of 1846. Few cities in the nation showed such unambiguous distaste for the protracted Viet Nam war as Boston, scene of draft-card burnings, protest demonstrations, and even State House legislation declaring the war unjust and unconstitutional.

Youthful City
Many American cities have automatic, knee-jerk associations.

Pittsburgh, for example, means *steel*, Akron *rubber*, Nashville *music*, and Grand Rapids *furniture*. But what of Boston? Nowadays nobody thinks seriously of the noble codfish. More than anything, Boston today is a student city, a youthful city.

Boston itself and its suburbs comprise an extraordinary concentration of colleges, junior colleges, and universities. Within twenty miles from the State House are fifty-six degree-granting institutions and a number of private preparatory schools. Several universities have budgets comparable to large corporations. Both Harvard and M.I.T., for example, have annual budgets of over two hundred million dollars and attract students from all over the world.

Ride one of Boston's subway or trolley cars at any hour of the day and the chances are it will be at least one-third filled with book-carrying students. One of my Vermont acquaintances, reflecting on his four years of college in Boston, wonders whether he didn't gain more from *experiencing* Boston than from his structured, required college courses. Of course not all college students like Boston, but most of them do.

Boston's large student population is almost equaled by thousands of young people who are *unofficial* students. No longer registered in any college, they nonetheless study peace, nutrition, Eastern philosophy, the principles of Zen, transcendental meditation, feminism, or black history either individually or in informal collectives. Some are proud college dropouts who feel they learn more on their own. Others are from various parts of the country, lured to the city at about the time a national magazine featured Boston as the "No. 1 City of Young."

Altogether this youthful population gives Boston a certain verve; in turn, the city treats its young with more tolerance than in most American cities. True, Boston police sometimes like to rout "hippies" from Boston Common, but as more moustached and long-haired recruits join the Boston Police, such "hippie roundups" are becoming rarer. Besides, these engaging young people can shake up the establishment. When Boston solemnly reenacted the Boston Tea Party on its 200th anniversary, Boston's antic young staged their own counter-demonstration in the harbor and stole most of the headlines and TV coverage.

The Boston Accent

America is a nation of regional accents and Boston is no exception. To an English person, the entire country speaks "the mother tongue" in a peculiar way, at least if English as spoken on the BBC is the standard. Probably America's southern accent, of which there are many variants, is the most noticeable accent. President Lyndon Johnson spoke with an unmistakable Texan twang, but his predecessor was often kidded about his Boston accent, sometimes by New Yorkers blissfully unaware of the hard, harsh "d's" and "t's" of their own regional speech.

In truth, President Kennedy's Boston accent was combined with an elitest, private-school argot, but the Boston speech was instantly recognizable. Thus he would omit the sound of the letter "r" in some words, so that "park" became "pahk" and "car" became "cah", while adding an "r" sound where it didn't belong: "Cuba" became "Cuber" and "America" became "Americar." Most native Bostonians speak this curious way. Drive into Boston from the west and ask a toll-booth attendant west of the city what the toll is and he'll say "fawty" (meaning "forty") or a "quawtah" (meaning "quarter"). North of Boston, up in Maine and New Hampshire, the accent is even more pronounced. I do not claim that the Boston accent is one of the city's charms. In fact, I am amazed that native Californians, so far removed from England compared with Boston, speak a more acceptable English. But at least it contributes to the valid idiosyncracy of the city.

Suburban Recreation

What city isn't a blend of a core city and surrounding areas? One of Boston's assets is that wilderness trails, ski areas, and unbroken miles of sandy beach lie close to the central city. Just south of Boston in neighboring Milton and Canton is the Blue Hills Reservation with winter skiing as well as miles of hiking and bridle trails. True, the ground is occasionally covered with bullet-holed beer cans, discarded auto batteries, and the usual cigarette and candy wrappings so characteristic of America, but there are also sunny, rocky ledges with blueberries, and hills with a magnificent view of the city and its island-fringed harbor.

North of the city the Lynn woods—a large expanse of land ideal for hikers, joggers, bird-watchers, cross-country skiers, and strollers—can be reached within thirty minutes by train. Near Winchester, a "bedroom community" six miles north of Boston, is the Middlesex Fells Reservation. Scout troops hike here, the Winchester High School cross-country team slices through the woods in practice and meet, and young people—to the distress of patrolling police—sometimes swim nude in the reservoirs on hot summer nights.

Of course, the best swimming around Boston is on the many beaches north and south of the city. Revere Beach, with its honky-tonk atmosphere of cheap nightclubs, pizza stands, and roller coasters is considered *déclassé*, but a new breed of young Bostonians, free of their parents' class consciousness, find the tacky place campy and convenient—a fifteen-minute, twenty-five-cent subway-elevated ride from Boston. (Alas, the amusement park and pizza stands are giving way to seaside apartment houses and condominiums.) Just beyond is a better beach at

Lynn, a long expanse of sand and rock with Boston's skyline as a backdrop. In general, the surf is gentle enough for ocean swimming and sharks seldom venture into such cool northern waters.

Newspapers

At one time Boston was noted for its ability to support half a dozen daily newspapers, each appealing to a particular demographic or political group. The "Proper Bostonian," for example, could read the *Evening Transcript*, while the *Post* was read by chauffeur and maid. Both of these newspapers have disappeared, along with others, leaving Boston with three papers, two of them excellent—the *Boston Globe* and the *Christian Science Monitor*. Strictly speaking, the *Monitor* is not a Boston newspaper, but an international daily newspaper sold the world over and printed and published in Boston, which represents only a small percentage of its circulation. Still, it is a daily newspaper and its principal editors are Bostonians.

It is the *Boston Globe* which is building a reputation as one of America's fine newspapers. Once an ordinary newspaper known hardly beyond the metropolitan area, the *Globe*, with its Asian bureau and host of Washington reporters, now rates among America's best. Some of this is due to the paper's investigative reporting, for the *Globe* likes to probe below the surface. It has taken on some mighty "sacred cows" and editorially supported unpopular causes such as general amnesty for Viet Nam war resisters. True, the *Globe* eventually fired its radical columnist, David Deitch, ostensibly for writing for an opposing periodical, but in effect for having expressed heretical views on real estate developers, banks, and insurance companies.

Such big corporations are more aggressively dealt with in several weeklies, such as the *Phoenix* and *The Real Paper*, which

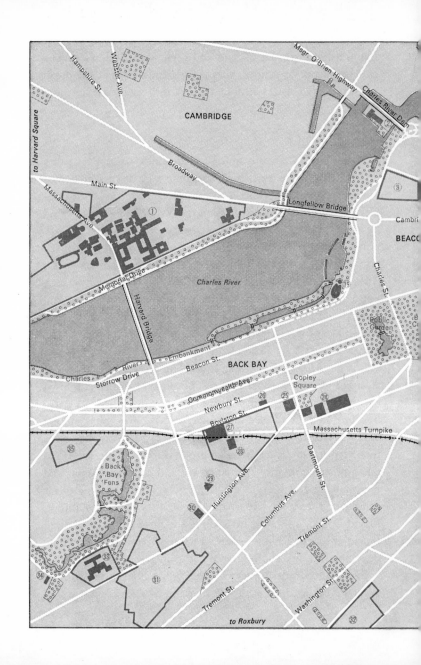

CENTRAL BOSTON

have had hard-hitting pieces on negligence in the building industry, prejudice practiced by prestigious firms, and real estate shenanigans. As good a daily paper as it is, even the *Globe* has occasionally found itself picking up the trail blazed by one of these irreverent weeklies, which do not depend on large banks, retail stores, and establishment figures for their advertising support. The weeklies are sold on street corners all over Boston. Once read only by students or young people and filled with stereo and record ads, they're increasingly reaching a wider audience and forcing the conventional dailies to become less reactionary in their news coverage.

Boston as a Medical Center

When stomach surgery performed on Sir Anthony Eden in London failed to restore him to adequate health, he embarrassed his eminent British surgeons by crossing the Atlantic and placing himself in the hands of Boston doctors, for the city has a reputation as the world's greatest medical center. The Shah of Iran brought an entourage, including his own chefs, when he came to Boston for treatment. Even New Yorkers have been known to leave their own city to avail themselves of Boston medicine.

This international reputation is at least partly due to Harvard Medical School, perhaps the country's finest, to Massachusetts General Hospital, a sprawling complex on the bank of the Charles River, and the Lahey Clinic, whose waiting rooms are filled with people from all over the United States and Canada. Several Presidents, including Franklin Roosevelt and John F. Kennedy, have been patients at this private clinic.

Some cities such as Houston which pride themselves on their advanced medical resources feel Boston medicine is too conservative, for no pioneering heart transplants have taken place there. Occasional medical students at Cleveland's Western Reserve will refer to Boston's medical fraternity as traditional. There is a wholesome truth to both observations, for Boston's reputation has been built on solid medical practice and research that scorns unnecessary surgery. Nevertheless, Boston has always had brilliant surgeons who have attracted patients from all over the world.

The Children's Medical Center has done pioneering work in the treatment of juvenile cancer, and the Massachusetts General Hospital (where the X ray was developed) has saved the lives of many cancer patients with controlled use of drugs combined with radiation therapy. Nobody likes to be ill, but if it should happen to you in Boston and you can afford the best medical treatment in the world, you'll find it right at hand.

THE BOSTON MASSACRE 1770

THE CITY CHANGES

For a while in the fifties and sixties, hundreds of old Boston buildings were being torn down in the name of urban renewal. Neighborhoods were either being sliced in half or (like Chinatown) bordered with new arterial roads. But gradually a new sense of "the Boston image" began to permeate the city's private and public sectors. Boston still has no landmarks preservation commission, and some fine old buildings like the huge South Station are destined for destruction. But at last the city realizes that its supply of old buildings is not limitless.

Few American cities would retain an old city hall once a new one had been built and occupied, but Boston is no ordinary city; as soon as a new city hall had been announced, efforts were begun to retain the old one. The basic premise—one that has saved many a Boston building—was that in a time of rising costs and scarcity of building materials, money could be saved by remodeling a sound structure and giving it a new use. Of course more than money is saved: the substance and spirit of a community is preserved. Long before the new city hall at Government Center had been completed, Bostonian Roger Webb organized the Old City Hall Landmark Corporation to breathe new life into the old place. Today this remodeled city hall has private and state offices, a bank, and a brick-walled French restaurant which spills outside for seasonal outdoor dining. With a unique financial arrangement, the recycled building is producing revenue for the city in a novel way: in place of taxes, the city will collect more than twenty-five million dollars in rentals from its ninety-nine-year lease to the corporation.

Although historic preservation is underway in many parts of Boston, perhaps the most dramatic restoration is the city's waterfront. A dozen years ago the wharf area was a moribund commercial section vacated at night and only half busy by day since the port of Boston operated far below capacity. When people talked then of waterfront development, they spoke of razing old buildings for new improved roads and piers and more parking.

But the waterfront developed its own way. Despite a six-lane expressway which places an unaesthetic barrier between the waterfront and the rest of the city, the harbor area has suddenly become an eminently desirable residential area. A few artistic people had always lived there, appreciating gulls, harbor sunrises, and fishing trawlers coming in to dock. Its other residents in nearby lofts were not attracted by the waterfront: they just liked reasonable rents in the decaying commercial neighborhood. Now all is changing as spacious lofts and warehouses are purchased by wealthy people and corporations with grander ideas.

Not everyone is pleased with the changes taking place along the waterfront. Consider the comment of a former tenant who had to move when a California-based company purchased the old Gardner building where he lived to make it into a restaurant: "The old commercial, colorful waterfront had to make way for a glamorous new waterfront. It's as if they're replacing the real heart of the waterfront with a steel one."

New residents, however, some living in forty-thousand-dollar condominiums, like not only the nautical flavor but also the area's closeness to the central city. Waterfront residents can walk to work, step out to a fine restaurant within a few blocks, and enjoy Boston's theater without worrying about catching the 12:10 train to Concord.

Fortunately, the harborside has grown not only residentially but commercially. Massport, which operates both Boston's air and sea ports, admits that until recently an ocean-going passenger ship was about as rare a sight in Boston Harbor as on the Platte River in Nebraska. But the city has jumped from total obscurity on passenger sailing schedules to fifth place among American major deep-water passenger-ship ports. With a refurbished Commonwealth Pier, sailings for the Caribbean, Europe, the Mediterranean, Canada, and Bermuda are now on the increase and the port is winning back business it had lost to more progressive ports which adapted to containerized shipping sooner. It is hardly an exaggeration to refer to it as a port reborn.

A healthier waterfront, the nearby North End, and genteel Beacon Hill perhaps give the impression that all is well with Boston housing. But the city has decaying neighborhoods and problems which I have no intention of glossing over, even if most of them are endemic to American cities.

Many of the city's problems developed when prosperous families left their city homes for the suburbs, followed by many a business. Decline in tax revenue and the deterioration of buildings resulted. Municipal services waned, once fine homes on tree-lined Commonwealth Avenue became either morose rooming houses with fraying window curtains or well-appointed medical suites for Boston's prestigious doctors. (It's been said that doctors are to Boston as priests are to the Vatican.) In other sections of the city, particularly in Roxbury and Dorchester, the great suburban migration had more devastating results. Owners of city buildings, themselves happy on the rolling suburban acres of Wayland or Dover, allowed their city properties to decline while they simultaneously raised rentals. Massive changes in the character of neighborhoods was inevitable.

Not long ago Francis Russell, a former resident of Dorchester, returned to find "ramshackle houses, empty houses, ruined houses, the yards overgrown with ragweed and ankle deep in debris." Frankly, large areas of Boston appear decimated and street crime is not uncommon.

Approximately fifty thousand Spanish-speaking people now live in Dorchester, many of them Puerto Ricans who've moved north from New York in search of a better environment. There has also been a recent influx from crowded Santo Domingo in the Dominican Republic. Unlike New York, Boston doesn't have daily Spanish-language newspapers or full-time Spanish radio stations, so some of these Hispanic people feel even more isolated in the Boston culture where Spanish is seldom used.

In some dilapidated buildings along Dudley Street in Dorchester, people who speak little English find themselves victims of the same sort of discrimination which the Irish felt a generation ago. A recent arrival who had come up from New York ("too many people and too many junkies in New York") was surprised at the prejudice in Boston. Some efforts are being made to have Spanish-speaking people in municipal offices and more school instruction in Spanish. But Boston is slow to absorb its new Hispanic residents.

Lately an influx of young people into Boston has had a salutary effect on many neighborhoods. Buying tumbledown, distressed properties, they have begun to fix them up. These thousands of young people may yet change the face of the city. The *New York Times*, noting the migration of young people "to gray old Boston town," said: "At times, it seems like the streets are vast rivers flowing with blue denim, hair, ski parkas—

the uniform of an exuberant youthful army that is profoundly altering the social complexion of this once staid old center of Brahmin propriety." Contrary to popular myth, most of these young people are not penniless "hippies" who live off welfare. An astonishing number of young professionals—lawyers, doctors, dentists, journalists, teachers—have moved to the city from all over America. Their *concern* for a wholesome life-style supplies a proper balance to those exponents of "progress" who still want to tear down to build anew. Saving buildings, encouraging farmers to bring in fresh produce from nearby farms, running for city offices, working in newspaper and television stations, they are having an influence far beyond their numbers. Together with long-term Boston residents, they are not afraid of social action and challenging hitherto unquestioned attitudes. Thus Boston is a city where the feminist current is stronger than in most cities. For example, when women workers at the Boston Redevelopment Authority noted that male workers doing exactly the same work were paid more, they rightly went to court and won their case.

Writing articles, filing lawsuits, picketing at various sites, Bostonians are today protesting pollution of the Charles River, the building of skyscrapers, recently outlawed segregation practiced in Boston's public schools, and the growth of the private automobile at the expense of public transportation. They are even challenging New England's use of the sea, something that has always been taken for granted. In short, many Bostonians are so concerned with their environment that ultimately they may have as much influence on Boston as the Brahmins did in the last century.

For all its faults, patrician Boston is now one of America's more sensible cities, and one of its more interesting. At one time young executives in various parts of the United States used to look forward to ultimate achievement: transfer to New York and corporate headquarters. Today the city one angles for is Boston, that immensely livable city on the sea.

APPENDIX

Hotels

If you dislike, as I do, the new plastic hotels cropping up all over America, complete with hollow and fake beams in their "Olde English Pubs," I would suggest you consider several places, none of which belongs to the plasticized, impersonal "hotel-modern" school. If you have plenty of money, stay at the still elegant Ritz Carleton and ask for a room overlooking the Public Garden across the street. However, if you're not properly dressed for the Ritz (perhaps you're wearing jeans, a jellaba you purchased in Marrakech, or too brief a miniskirt), the Ritz can treat you with insufferable coolness.

You might be interested to know that Boston is still a theatrical "tryout town." Plays ultimately headed for a Broadway opening in New York often have a two-week run in Boston before moving into New York where opening-night drama critics can make or break a production after one performance. The Ritz Carleton has traditionally been the home of theater people and especially playwrights who have been known to rewrite plays completely in Ritz rooms before a New York debut. Many a three-act play has opened at Boston's Colonial Theater only to enter New York a fortnight later as a trim two-act piece.

The Ritz is not only located across the street from a tree-filled public park complete with a four-acre lake and well-known Swan Boats, it is adjacent to the quaint shops, art galleries, antique stores, boutiques, and bookstores of fashionable Newbury Street. Despite a vestigial stuffiness once common to much of Boston, the Ritz makes an ideal place to stay.

On a more moderate budget, you might consider two other vintage hotels. After all, since you are in an old city, you might as well try to *feel* some of this past even if a once proud hotel has declined and its plumbing is temperamental, its rugs frayed, its plaster flaking away! If you insist on modern hotels, go to Springfield, Worcester, or to some city like Indianapolis where *all* old downtown hotels have been razed. Fortunately, Boston's famous Parker House still stands in an old part of Boston near the impressive state capitol building on Beacon Hill. The list of people who have stayed in this hotel would read like a *Who's Who*. When the Dunfey family took over this deteriorating hotel, Senator Edward M. Kennedy recalled at a reception that on his first visit to downtown Boston, his father took him to a lunch of Boston schrod at the Parker House—home of the famous Parker House rolls. Today this hotel has whole floors reserved for airline crews staying overnight, but Boston's oldest operating hotel deserves support and is ideally situated for a walking tour of historic Boston.

Like the Parker House, the Copley Plaza Hotel has new management. At first it was renamed The Sheraton Plaza, but the Sheraton Corporation was astute enough to realize that old names die hard in Boston and wisely gave it back its old name. (The Sheraton hotel chain has its world headquarters in Boston at the site of the famous Boston Tea Party at the edge of the harbor.) The vintage Copley Plaza, with a pleasant plaza in front, is right near what is considered architecturally one of the most interesting buildings in Boston, the stately Boston Public Library, facing Copley Square. If you *must* have an up-to-date hotel, there is a modern Sheraton-Boston nearby. Its top four floors are especially luxurious and offer, I must admit, a more far-ranging view of Boston than from any of my recommended hotels! If you have an outside room facing north, you may be astonished when the bellman opens the curtains of your expansive, windowed wall to reveal the low rooftops of Back Bay buildings below you, the Charles River with its bridges beyond, and the university city of Cambridge on the other side of the river.

Restaurants
Fortunately, Boston is one of the better restaurant cities on the East Coast and is especially well known for its seafood restaurants, a number of which are located right on the harbor. It has its share of "vintage restaurants," as Edburnne Hare, a writer for *Boston* magazine, calls them—old places which, like some of my recommended hotels, have been around awhile. For a light meal, Stuart Street near the theater district offers Jacob Wirth's, familiarly known since 1868 as Jake Wirth's. Like many restaurants around Boston, it is an unpretentious place which you could pass by on the street without noticing. As more than one restaurant reviewer has noted, this is an old-fashioned place whose only concession to time has been electricity, air-conditioning, and occasional paper napkins. Wirth's is noted among students for its seidels of dark beer and its mahogany bar, hardly altered over a century. Some of its waiters *seem* almost that old. The lentil soup is recommended, along with Bismark herring; for carnivores, there's roast beef and sausage, with sauerbraten.

Durgin Park is probably the most interesting historic restaurant in Boston. No place for a quiet tête à tête, for there are huge long tables where everyone sits family style like a German beer hall. The tables, covered with red-checkered tablecloths, have huge pitchers of water, refilled by hefty, strong-voiced waitresses who've been compared with truckdrivers. Connoisseurs of small, dark, hushed restaurants are advised to steer clear of this incredible restaurant which treats longshore workers, tourists, and Boston politicians the same. There are no reservations and no private tables, but plenty of good seafood—oysters, shellfish, clams, and about every kind of fish from nearby Atlantic waters. For dessert, have strawberry shortcake, Indian pudding made with good molasses, or apple pan dowdy.

Union Oyster House, like nearby Durgin Park, is old, dating back to 1826. Originally, the building was the former home of an exiled French king, then briefly a drygoods store before becoming a fine restaurant. But be alert—that "waterboy" who provides your table with water, bread, and butter just might be a college president! Union Oyster House was where a distinguished college president from Pennsylvania recently took his sabbatical leave. President John Coleman of Haverford College didn't want to languish in London attending the theater; he wanted to see what life was like among America's working class in 1973. When he applied for a restaurant job dressed in weathered clothing used for his gardening hobby, nobody thought to ask him if he were a college graduate, let alone if he were a college president. So, as a kitchen salad man and substitute busboy, he quickly learned that most restaurant patrons felt immeasurably superior to him, an observation later confirmed when, as a garbage collector, he couldn't get anyone to reply to his cheery "Good morning!" as he made the rounds.

A more traditional restaurant is Locke-Ober Café, which celebrated its 100th birthday in 1973. Women have been attempting to liberate its men's bar so that both sexes may enjoy a stand-up aperitif and I hope they succeed. For years "Locke Obers" has been regarded as Boston's preeminent restaurant. Its only disadvantage is that it is situated at the dead end of Winter Place and offers no view along with the meal.

Recently, two restaurants close to the harbor have attracted attention along with expense-account diners and tourists. Bostonians are forever debating the merits of these two restaurants, both on Northern Avenue. Anthony's Pier 4 is more impressive, with a vessel berthed right next to the restaurant so you can have a shipboard cocktail before walking down the gangplank to the restaurant with its magnificent harbor view. Down the street is Jimmy's Harbor Side, well patronized by Boston's advertising fraternity. Both restaurants serve excellent seafood. I happen to prefer Jimmy's, but there are some Bostonians who patronize neither and recommend their own special discoveries. Thus author and *Atlantic* editor, Dan Wakefield, who abandoned his home city of Indianapolis to live in Boston, prefers Stella's, an Italian restaurant in the North End; and radio executive Mike Horn has been known to take clients across the river to Cambridge and Legal Sea Foods.

BRITISH EVACUATING BOSTON 1776

51. *Preceding page*, from mid-April until late September, the Boston Red Sox attract loyal fans to Fenway Park in the Back Bay.

52. *Opposite*, Boston is a preeminent theater "tryout" city. Plays hopefully headed for long runs in New York have preliminary tryouts, often resulting in revisions, in Boston. The Colonial Theater is one of the city's best known.

53-54. In late spring, Symphony Hall, home of the famous Boston Symphony Orchestra, takes on a lighter air. The musical event is the Boston Pops, and tables are set up for refreshments.

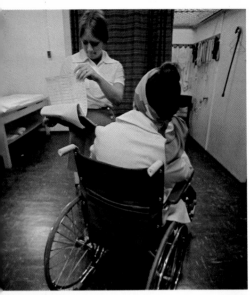

55. *Opposite*, for over a century, *The Atlantic Monthly* (now called simply *The Atlantic*) has been edited at offices on Arlington Street, opposite the Public Garden.

56–57. Massachusetts General Hospital: some consider Boston to be the world's foremost medical center.

58–59. *Opposite*, Cambridge Common, beside the campuses of Harvard and Radcliffe Colleges. *Opposite below*, Harvard College, the oldest in the United States, founded in 1636. Five American Presidents attended Harvard.

60–61. A scene on Cambridge Common, and a boutique near Harvard Yard.

62. *Overleaf*, in pleasant Sunday weather there's always free music to hear on Cambridge Common.

58

63. *Opposite*, Boston Harbor seen from a harbor cruise boat.
64. Yacht club on the Cambridge side of the Charles River, with a view of the Boston skyline.
65. Harvard students on a makeshift raft cruise the Charles River in May.

66–68. The Boston Fish Market. Boston is still a fishing port; fresh fish is flown from Boston to restaurants throughout the U.S.

69. *Overleaf*, the open-air food market in Haymarket Square, long a Boston tradition, continues to operate despite nearby building and highway construction.

70. *Opposite above*, customer at the Brattle Book Shop, America's oldest continually operating antiquarian bookstore, founded in 1825.

71. *Opposite below*, Boston is one of only seven American cities still to use sensible trolley cars.

72–73. Filene's is a large and attractive department store.

74–75. The tightly knit community called the "North End" is inhabited largely by Italian-Americans and contains some of the city's best Italian restaurants.

76. *Below*, a scene in Roxbury, several miles from the commercial center of the city.

77–79. MBTA (Massachusetts Bay Transit Authority) station at Dudley in the Roxbury section of Boston.

80. *Overleaf*, Revere Beach, a fifteen-minute subway ride to the north of Boston, is a popular spot during hot summer days.

81. Many of Boston's workers commute to suburban homes such as this one in Swampscott, a seaside "bedroom" community sixteen miles to the north.

THIS BEAUTIFUL WORLD